A History of
R.A.F. Station Harrowbeer
1944 to 1946

Air Ministry No. 23/341, August 1941 to July 1945

Dennis C. Teague A.R.Ae.S., F.I.M.M.

No. 276 Squadron Air Sea Rescue at dispersal with a Walrus and Defiant in blister pens and a Spitfire in the middle distance by the runway.

This version of the book is virtually as originally published, presenting the work of Dennis C Teague. There are now additional pages at the back providing information about the publisher, Arthur L Clamp.

The republishing project is being managed by Arthur's grandson, Steven Gibson. We aim to find all the research that he was involved in publishing, preserving it for the next generation as part of 'The Clamp Collection'.

Preface

In the early days of the War I was an A.T.C cadet and greeted the new aerodrome at Yelverton with great excitement as it held promise of different types of aircraft than those which operated from Roborough. I spent many hours there and any spare time that I had watching the fighters assembling for take off or returning from sweeps across the Channel. Unless one actually experienced the sight of a fighter unit formating, it is hard to describe. Prior to moving off each mighty Typhoon was cartridge-started and one could watch the pilot and ground crew firing up, a bang was followed by a puff of blue grey smoke until at last the huge four-bladed propellor churned around and the massive engine spluttered into life accompanied usually by a streak of flame and cloud of smoke. Each aircraft squeaked and groaned its way around until it was positioned for take off. Receiving the signal for the off, it roared down the runway and up into a sharp bank following the others and would join up in a large circle as many as 30 planes and whilst the last ones were taking off the pack would be droning around Burrator to Tavistock. Finally they would all form into a wedge shape and head off to the South East and the targets in the Channel Islands.

Harrowbeer was an active drome and whilst not on a par with some of the other bases along the South Coast it was always the home of at least one visiting Squadron in addition to the Air Sea Rescue unit and Communication units. It was very much multi-national and generally popular with the aircrews.

During the war it served the country well and now remains in peace having reverted to scrubland with only a stone to mark that it ever existed. This section is by no means intended as a complete history of the airfield or R.A.F. Station Harrowbeer but rather a compilation of data and remembered items.

Today when I go out to the Rock for a quiet drive or pass the old place by enroute to Chivenor, I still can see the aircraft at dispersal or streaming off; other times when it is quiet one can imagine aircraft taxiing around only to come back to reality and find that it is a lorry.

Harrowbeer may no longer exist but the memories do. I am still on the look out for anything that the readers may know of relating to any of the West Country airfields and would be pleased to hear from anyone who either served on these Stations or who may have photographs, etc.

D. C. Teague,
52 Beresford Street,
Stoke, Plymouth PL2 3AL

Additional Note

Shortly after my book *Aviation in South West Britain 1909-1979* had been published in 1982, I was approached by Mrs. O. Meggy who requested permission to use data from the book in a small booklet that she was preparing on Harrowbeer and she told me of the plans to erect a stone memorial to the wartime users of the airfield. Later on she told me of the information that she had collected and her hope to have it printed. Sadly Mrs. Meggy is no longer with us and I am therefore including her data with mine so that her ambition may be fulfilled.

Acknowledgements

I must record my many thanks to numerous people who gave information and loaned material for this publication. Among these are Wing Commander E. King, O.B.E., R.A.F. Rtd., Sqn. Ldr. R. F. Hamlyn, A.F.C., D.F.C., R.A.F., Rtd., Sqn. Ldr. Pearce, T. D. Jago, Lt. Col. R. A. Middleton and the Royal Air Force Museum at Hendon, London. Other photographs are from the author's collection, R. Cottey, J. Westlake, Polish and Czech pilots stationed here during the war. Many photographs are also from private collections such as the Harrowbeer Memorial Committee.

The Author

Although now almost completely gone, Harrowbeer is well remembered by many who served here and by local residents. I hope this illustrated account will bring back memories and recall times of challenge, uncertainty and friendship between people of different nations brought together to fight the common enemy.

Ready for the fight: A Typhoon "E" of B Flight, No. 193 Squadron, is photographed at Harrowbeer sometime in 1942/43 with Pilot Vernon Jarvis in the centre and, left, airframe mechanic Phillips and, right, engine mechanic R. E. Tudball.

Royal Air Force Station Harrowbeer Devon

There can be few other airfields, if any, which were built on the rubble of the place they were designed to protect from enemy bombing but this was the case with Harrowbeer. Today one can be forgiven if you go right past it without ever knowing that it existed at all. Leaving Plymouth, on the north road, and heading for Tavistock and Launceston some seven miles from the City centre, the road which has been almost straight sweeps around and then goes down hill to Yelverton roundabout.

It is on this stretch on the left hand side that one will see a large rock outcrop and further on the same side some grassy mounds usually covered in litter. The roundabout was the end of one runway and, bearing left to go to Tavistock, a few buildings can be seen before the road sweeps past other buildings comprising the hamlet of Harrowbeer.

It hardly seems possible that a busy airfield once existed on this desolate scrubland and, even more surprising, that a very bitter conflict was waged post war when it was proposed as the logical Plymouth city airport.

Looking at the wilderness there is no doubt as to which side won, the champions of the desolation who adopted the attitude that it was alright for young servicemen and women to give their lives fighting to maintain the standard of life but no way were the noisey aircraft going to be allowed to operate post war airline services.

Harrowbeer was born out of a cross between need and forward planning. As a site for a Fighter Command airfield it was planned for 1941 operational life and the land acquired in the late 1930s. Opposition to these plans was notably absent when faced with invasion. 1941 saw the almost total destruction of Plymouth and this spurred on the construction of the new airfield. Great quantities of rubble from the blitzed city was brought out and used to form the hardcore for the runways. Construction was fairly straight forward and throughout the rest of the year workmen cleared the scrubland to laydown the standard 'A' type configuration of runways. No mention of Harrowbeer can be made without the *Rock*, an outcrop which rises rather like a dark pillow to the southern end of the runways. The two runways crossed in front of it and although it was such a frightening object no one ever made contact with it.

The first building to be constructed was a corrugated iron *blister* hangar on land adjacent to the Rock. This with a large house, which still exists today called *Ravenscroft*, was the start of occupation. The house became the station H.Q. and was fully occupied until the end of the war. It then was vacated and for several years was the target of the *Polish Gold* hunters. A story had got around that when the Polish Forces set up again in Britain they had brought with them vast amounts of gold and silver objects from their churches and had buried it on one of the British airfields that they served upon. The result of this rumour was amazing, everywhere the Poles had been and this included in the South West, Culmhead, Exeter, Predannack, Davidstow Moor and Harrowbeer, small units of diggers were to be noted leaving a trail of destruction behind them. *Ravenscroft* and its grounds were quite badly damaged. Another semi-circular hangar was erected with bombing dispersals near the Rock and the control tower more or less completed the south western corner. Some stores were built up in the north west corner and a hospital organised but all on a small scale.

The first aircraft to land was a 500 Squadron Blenheim If bomber which stood outside the blister hangar. A few days later several more arrived these being Blenheims Mk. Ifs which were fighters and it is assumed that these were on detachment from their base and probably were being used either as escorts for the Sunderland flying boats at R.A.F. Mount Batten. V.I.Ps were taken to the Middle East and had fighter protection for part of the way or possible alternative use as a trials unit for the new airfield. Not long after their arrival one machine crashed onto a lorry carrying ground crews with several casualties.

During September, 1941, a number of Hurricanes moved in possibly from an operational training unit. These sported various colour schemes but carried no codes, only single letters and included one in pre-Battle of Britain colours. The size of the airfield compared with the number of aircraft using it was laughable. However, all this was to change quite large aircraft did land usually on weather diversions or emergency landings. Harrowbeer was not a bomber base and the sightings of Halifax and Stirlings has given rise to very strange accounts of hundreds of American bombers taking off and even reports from crews who state that they flew operations in bombers from there (these turned out to be Coastal Command Liberators from Chivenor, north Devon). The station at no time operated bombers although one did manage to force land right alongside the main road near the Rock. One large transport Harrow used to fly in and out on communications as did many Oxford and Ansons. New residents in October, 1941, were Spitfire operational status fighters of No. 130 Squadron known as the *Pubjab* who stayed until November and the much longer remaining 276 Squadron Air Sea Rescue Unit which commenced their stay until May, 1943. The Squadron was formed at Harrowbeer on the 21st October and operated Defiant, Spitfire, Lysander and Walrus aircraft.

November saw the arrival of Polish Spitfire Vbs of No. 302 Squadron under Sqn. Ldr. Kowalski which stayed until May, 1942. The Poznan Squadron also served at Culmhead on the Somerset border with Devon. This Station was also known as *Churchstanton* and it was from here that they came to Harrowbeer as did several other R.A.F. Squadrons made up of pilots from many nations who had escaped. The West Country was host to Polish, Czech, French and Belgian Squadrons plus units from the Dutch and Norwegian, our own Royal Australian, Canadian, New Zealand Squadrons and the U.S. Navy/Army Air Forces. All these were part of an impressive total of 286 units known to have served at one time or another during the War and shortly afterwards in this country.

1942: The building continued and Harrowbeer began to resemble an operational Station. Sqn. Ldr. Cermak with No. 312 Czech Squadron with Spitfire Vcs replaced in May, 1942, the Poles of 302. Up to this date, April 1942, St. Eval in Cornwall had been a Sector Station controlling the fighter aircraft at Plymouth Roborough and the airfields at Perranporth, Portreath, Predannack and St. Marys. Now with the Battle of Britain over new areas were formed not so much for defence but attack.

President H. Truman at a window of his private aircraft *The Sacred Cow*. His plane was diverted to R.A.F. Harrowbeer upon returning from the historic Potsdam Conference in Berlin just after the war.

Royal Air Force Units based at R.A.F. Harrowbeer

Squadron Number	Type	Code letters	Dates
1	Spitfire LF IX	JX	June to August 1944.
26	Mustang IV	JX	April to May 1945.
26	Spitfire XIV	XC	June, 1944 to May, 1945.
64	Spitfire IX	SH	June to August 1944.
126	Spitfire IX	5J	July to Sept 1944.
130	Spitfire II	PJ	October to November 1941.
131	Spitfire VII	NX	March to May 1944.
165	Spitfire IX		May 1944.
175	Hurricane IIb	HH	October to December 1942.
183	Typhoon Ia	HF	June to August 1943.
193	Typhoon Ib	DP	December, 1942 to March, 1943.
263	Whirlwind F.1	HE	February to March 1943.
263	Typhoon	HE	March to June 1944.
266	Typhoon Ib	ZH	September, 1943 to March, 1944.
275	Walrus	PV	January to February 1945.
276	Lysander, Defiant, Spitfire	AQ	October, 1941 to 3 April, 1944. April to July 1945.
279	Hudson A.S.R. II		June, 1943 to November, 1943.
302 Polish	Spitfire Vb	WX	November, 1941 to May, 1942
312 Czech	Spitfire Vb	DU	May to October 1942.
329 Free French	Spitfire IX	5A	May to June 1945, last unit.
340	Spitfire IX	GW	
414 Canadian	Mustang Ib	RU	1943 May to June.
456 Australian	Mosquito		
500	Blenheim IVL		September to October 1941, B Flight.
610	Spitfire XVI	DW	May to June 1944.
611	Spitfire LF Vb	FY	June to July 1944.
691	Oxford, Vengeance	5S	January to August 1945.
838 Royal Navy	Swordfish FAA		April to August 1944.

It is not generally realised that during the Battle of Britain period the South West was fully stretched defence wise as was the Eastern sector of the country. Spitfire and Hurricane units, operating from as far apart as the Isles of Scillies to Warmwell, were in action throughout the period and did much to minimise enemy raids on inland targets. St. Eval, now extinct, alongside R.A.F. St. Mawgan, provided Spitfire, Hurricane and Blenheim fighters. Roborough had Gladiators and later Hurricanes, Exeter and Warmwell had Hurricane and Spitfire Squadrons. The new organisation made Exeter the Sector Section with Bolt Head as a forward landing airfield. Aircraft could be drawn on from Churchstanton/Culmhead, Exeter or Harrowbeer and the normal pattern of events was to organise and mount an attack from Bolt Head using fighter bombers from Harrowbeer such as Whirlwinds with strong fighter cover using the aircraft from Exeter and Culmhead.

Late October saw the arrival of No. 175 with Hurricane IIbs which were the fighter bomber version of these famous fighters and almost at once were engaged upon attacks upon enemy shipping. Targets in the Channel Islands and along the French coast were subjected to low level strikes. One of the Squadron's successes came when they intercepted three *E* boats. These very high speed torpedo boats had earned a reputation around the coasts and had wrecked havoc amongst not only the merchant shipping but the escorts as well. Well armed, they engaged without fear up to destroyers and when the Hurribombers were directed on to three of them the odds were against the aircraft. They were armed with one 37mm cannon, one twin 20mm and one single 20mm each of the three put up a barrage of fire, heavier and at greater range than the Hurricanes could reply to. It was no mean feat to bomb and sink two and badly damage a third of the boats.

December 18th, 1942, was a turning point in the story of Harrowbeer for it was on that day that No. 193 Squadron was formed on the Station with the new Typhoon fighters which were to be based there for another two years. These aircraft were kept as far away as possible from the public road and normally parked over in *Tiffy Corner* which was the westward limit of the north west corner and they were dispersed as far in the blast shelters as was possible. The Typhoon was a very fine aircraft but suffered a very high casualty rate due to an engine which failed to come up to expectations. The Typhoon was a snub-nosed design with all the weight up in the front and a troublesome engine made take off and landings very difficult to cope with in the early days. The cartridge start was prone to catching fire and yet, once mastered, the *Tiffy* could be flown superbly. It did not meet its design intention as a high altitude interceptor and so was tried out

Ready for take off, a Westland twin-engined Whirlwind of No. 263 Squadron, is powered by two 885 hp Rolls Royce engines. The plane is equipped with four 20mm cannons and can carry two 500lb bombs.

in the reverse role of a low level fighter bomber. The early machines had 12×303 machine guns but these were replaced by 4×20mm cannon and a new and probably the most deadly strike aircraft was born. Two underwing bombs of either 250 or 500lb delivered at high speed took their toll of shipping, installations and vehicles alike and Harrowbeer's aircraft were to be engaged upon this work for the next couple of years.

Several of the Station's aircraft came to grief, one hitting the nearby Church in May, 1944, at Yelverton whilst out on the Moors five others crashed. On the aerodrome itself four more were lost during take off and landings. The dangerous task they were undertaking also took a toll of the Station's aircraft during these days and many never returned.

February, 1943, after the trials of operating during the dark days, saw a Squadron which had very close ties with the South West. No. 263 arrived with their Whirlwinds. Since their formation 263 had served at Charmy Down, Bolt Head, Exeter, Portreath/Nanskuke and St.Eval. The Whirlwind was an excellent design, popular with most pilots but dogged with engine troubles and, therefore, not produced in numbers. It did perform well in the fighter bomber role and, escorted by fighters, played a useful part in strike attacks. Built at Westlands of Yeovil only two Squadrons were formed, 137 and 263, which were to lose their Whirlwinds at Harrowbeer and be re-equip with Typhoons which also had a history of engine troubles! During the month they made several anti-shipping attacks off the northern coast of France with these fast twin-engined fighters and during March, when they were converting to the Typhoons, many pilots expressed mixed feelings about them.

Harrowbeer has always been dubbed a *Typhoon Station* although this is strictly not true. However, 1943 saw another well known Squadron, No. 183 *Gold Coast*, arrive for another three month's residence and then No. 266 replaced them so for this year at least there were more of this type than anything else here, 193 spending all the year on Station under Wing Commander Butterworth.

A change of type had occurred in May when the Mustangs of 414 Squadron, Royal Canadian Air Force, *Imperial Squadron* being their title, also moved in for a period with a ground attack role. The Station was fully operational and a lot took place which now causes considerable difficulty to resolve. Buildings continued to be erected around the northern limits and then United States Naval staff arrived but for what reason still remains unclear. They were visited from time to time by their Catalina PBY 5A aircraft. An unidentified communications flight of U.S. machines lived down the Rock and comprised of Oxford and Spitfire aircraft with U.S. markings. During the period 1943-45 a great number of American light aircraft used the Station and many operational types diverted in until weather conditions improved. I recall seeing four all-white Hudson aircraft belonging to the Royal Canadian Air Force which were parked just inside the fence at what is known as *Leg of Mutton*, the buildings adjacent to the roundabout today. The unit is thought to be No. 407 Squadron.

In addition to the U.S. aircraft which diverted to the Station there were the odd few R.A.F. bombers which also landed for various reasons and created this myth about the Station being a Bomber base. A Halifax which overshot and ploughed up the gorse alongside the Rock, was on a flight from Gravely and put down late on the 28th February, 1943, and within hours the next day the rumour was spread that it was one of first of many four-engined aircraft to take up residence. It departed on several low loaders so exited W7906 of No. 35 Squardon and I expect the Germans were just as puzzled as to why the R.A.F. were reported to creating a bomber base in the West.

May or June, 1942: The Czech pilot, M.A.L. Liskutin, sits in his Spitfire Vb, EP559, of No. 312 Czech Squadron at Harrowbeer.

Another unconfirmed report was that there was several feet of rock removed from the top of the Rock itself the reason being given so that fully laden bombers could clear the top. This makes one wonder as Harrowbeer was designed for fighters.Transport and communication aircraft which were quite large did not have much trouble operating and quite a few of the twin-engined aircraft of Bomber Command and the U.S.A.A.F. could be seen from time to time, Bostons, Havoc, Marauder, Hampden, Wellington and Blenheims making short stays. A Stirling dwarfed everything else but that was overshadowed when the U.S. Liberator transports started using the Station along with PB5-YA from Dunkeswell.

Spitfires Everywhere

1944 saw a complete change of aircraft as the Typhoons departed to make way for Squadron after Squadron of Spitfires. Like all stations, Harrowbeer in 1944 was on top line for the allied invasion of Europe. The date was kept secret but there was no way of covering up that it was only a matter of time. The fighter bombers moved away nearer to where they were going to be needed and a mass of fighters gathered in the South West to provide cover and destroy any enemy aircraft attacks. Although the major threat to the ships crossing the Channel, the U Boat, had virtually been eliminated by Coastal Command and the Allied Navies no chance could be taken and so Fleet Air Arm anti-submarine aircraft started being deployed on R.A.F. bases. The big build up was under way.

February had seen No. 193 Squadron with their Typhoons depart followed in March by No. 266 likewise equipped. Arrivals started with No. 131 County of Kent Spitfire VII which left in May. The ensuing months saw a flood of Spitfire Squadrons make short stops including No. 610 which stayed with No. 263's Typhoons and the two Squadrons attacked targets in the Channel Islands on D Day. 131 with Spitfire Mk. VIIs, came in during March and they were joined by No. 340 *Ile de France* Free French Squadron in April which went to June. 131 had departed in late May.

The build up brought Nos. 1, 64, 165 and 611 Spitfire Squadrons for the 6th June, 1944, D Day and then these departed again by early July. The Station had served the purpose that it had been intended for and virtually died with the invasion.

July, 1944, saw No. 126 Squadron with Mustangs making a one month stay but by August with no future the Station was derated down to a satellite of Exeter. During the first half of 1944 Harrowbeer had enough based Spitfires to make up a wing and 48 took off one mid-day to attack enemy targets in France. Usually there were escorted attacks with bomb-carrying Typhoons escorted by Spitfires which used Bolt Head as Exeter's forward field.

As the War had moved away the Station had seen its Spitfires depart and the crews converting to Tempest and Meteors. 691 remained with Oxford and Vengeance aircraft up to the end of August, 276 remaining with their Walrus and a Sea Otter and the Free French Spitfire IX Squadron No. 329 having the honour of being the last operational fighter unit to use the airfield.

No. 130 Squadron, 1943

The propellors of a Spitfire II form the centre point of the Squadron's personnel grouped here for the photographer sometime during June, July or August, 1943, when it saw service at Harrowbeer. Many Squadrons served from this station, often for short periods of time; and hundreds of personnel passed through here like those shown.

Accidents at the Station

It is only natural that any drome had its share of crashes. There were many accidents which resulted from the cartridge start which, after more than three, there was a real danger of fire. Several machines skidded off the runways and tipped over plus the landing and take off failures. Typhoons, although excellent in the ground attacking straffing role, were prone to engine troubles. Examples of this being DN470 of 193 Squadron which crashed on landing 1943. DN510, same Squadron, crashed a short distance away. EK211 of 263 Squadron hit the Yelverton church tower in May, 1944, MN292, same Squadron, crashed at Launceston in June, 1944. 183 lost three aircraft, JP404 spun into ground, JP388 was damaged in an overshot when landing and JP393 burst a tyre on take off in July, 1943. 266 had JP962 which overshot and JR221 crashed in December, 1943, near Tavistock. A Mosquito crashed and exploded near Ravenscroft. Several Spitfires and visiting aircraft came to grief, and today the crews of these and those which failed to return from operations are remembered on the stone memorial located not far from the popular *Leg of Mutton* public house.

Gone, to be certain, but never to be forgotten by those from far and wide that served during the War years.

A Bolton Paul Defiant single engine aircraft is seen here in flight. It had a two man crew and was equipped with four rear-gun Browning .303s machine guns.

The Closing of the Station

Harrowbeer's operational life ended in July, 1945. However, Care and Maintenance status commenced a little later on. For a few years the airfield was kept on a non-operational footing but aircraft still made use of it such as units of the Army who exercised their Austers. Other service aircraft made touch and go landings which made one assume that the control towers were manned. On 2nd August a strange chain of events was to put Harrowbeer on the map as far as the press were concerned. It all started at Gatow when the Heads of State which had attended the world-shaping Potsdam Conference in Berlin were making their ways home.

President H. Truman of the United States was routed from Gatow to R.A.F. St. Mawgan, in Cornwall, the principal transit base for UK-USA transatlantic flights. His aircraft, a DC 4 called the *Sacred Cow*, departed at 0805 ten minutes after the first aircraft carrying the Secretary of State, J. Byrnes, had left, The third DC 4 with the remainder of the party followed on.

Fog now took a hand in the procedures and St. Mawgan was closed so the party of V.I.Ps were diverted to Harrowbeer which was clear and so the President touched down at 0940. The reception party were at St. Mawgan and only one officer, Lt. Col. Dewitt Greer, who was awaiting transport to St. Mawgan was there to welcome Mr. Truman.

King George VI was on board H.M.S. *Renown* which was at anchor in Plymouth Sound together with the U.S.S. *Augusta* and *Philadelphia*. The President was invited to have lunch with the King and boarded the U.S.S. *Augusta* at 1120. At 1235 the President, Secretary Byrnes and Admiral Leahy left the *Augusta* for *Renown* to call upon the King and were accorded the highest honours being personally escorted by the King. A return visit followed at 1504 when the King, Earl of Halifax, Sir Allen Lascalles called on the President. The King left at 1534 and fifteen minutes later the ships got under way.

In 1949 Harrowbeer reverted back to the scrubland so beloved by the preservationists. Dartmoor is a very emotive subject and any mention of any project to improve the lot of the nearby towns, such as badly needed reservoirs, send small groups into frenzied bursts of activity and public meeting get vast support from people living far outside the area. Harrowbeer will long be remembered both as an operational airfield and an opportunity lost.

1981 Stone Memorial

Finally the granite memorial to all those of wartime Harrowbeer which the *R.A.F. Harrowbeer Memorial Committee* had erected in 1981, serves as a worthwhile reminder of the past. The wording is:

R.A.F. Harrowbeer Operational 1941-49

From this Station flew pilots of many Commonwealth and Allied Countries including Britain, Canada, Czechoslovakia, France, Poland, Rhodesia and the United States of America with the support of their ground crews and Airfield Defence units.

This stone is in memory of all who served here and especially of those who gave their lives.

Many local residents helped build and maintain this airfield. Unveiled by the first Station Commander, Group Captain the Honourable E. F. Ward, on the 15th August, 1981, the fortieth anniversary of the opening of the Station.

Ravenscroft

This was the station's H.Q., officers' mess and quarters and is seen here as it looked during its wartime role. The building is still standing, it has been renovated to put to other uses.

In the Cockpit

This close view of the pilot and cockpit of a Spitfire clearly shows the headgear worn, the head rest behind the pilot and his oxygen mask. Seen here is Sqn. Ldr. R. F. Hamlyn, A.F.C., D.F.C., Commanding Officer of No. 276 Squadron.

C.O.'s Office

This sparsely furnished room at Ravenscroft was the station commander's office and, no doubt, will hold memories for many ranks when news of returning and loss of aircraft and crews was made known from here.

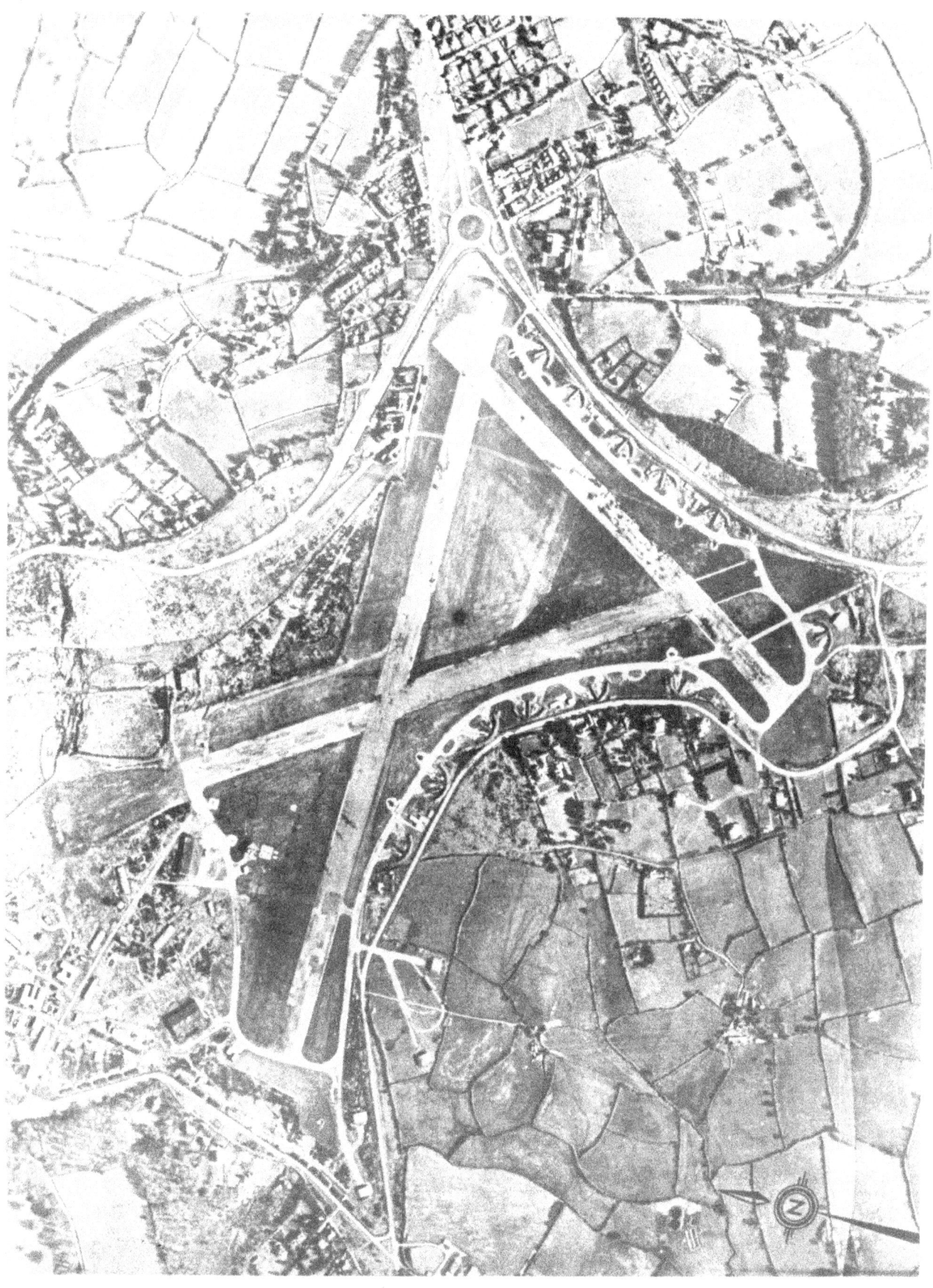

Harrowbeer airfield as likely seen by pilots flying to and from home showing the distinctive X-shaped plan of the runways with eleven blast pens on the edge of the field. They would have given some protection to static aircraft if Harrowbeer had been attacked by enemy aircraft. The main road from Plymouth to Tavistock skirts the airfield just to its right with Yelverton roundabout half way along.

TARGETS ATTACKED	126 Sq	64 Sq	611	TOTAL WING
DEST.	3FW190 5ME109	2 ME109		3FW190 8ME109 1 DO217(G)
E/A Pr.Dest.	1 UTE (G) 1 ME109	—	/	1 U.TE(G) 1 ME109
DAM.	2 ME109 4 JU88 (G)	—	/	4 JU88(G) 2 ME109
LOCOS.	16	2	5	23
RAIL TRUCKS DEST + DAM	40	79	30	149
M.T. Vehicles DEST + DAM	78	54	47	179
A.F.V.S.	1	—	7	8
Shipping DEST + DAM (TONS)	210	630	300	1140
Installations				

This very interesting Harrowbeer score board records some of the successes achieved by two Squadrons operating from here in late August, 1944. A list of enemy targets is given on the left and the numbers of noted hits chalked on the board. Pilot "Sammy" Samuels is at the controls of a Typhoon named *Salome* ready here for another sortie from Harrowbeer sometime in 1943.

Loading a Spitfire IIc

This plane was the Air Sea rescue version of the Spitfire IIc and is seen here probably being loaded with marker flares to be dropped to indicate the position of crew who had ditched into the sea. The plane belonged to No. 276 Squadron.

No. 691 Squadron operated Fairey Barracuda aircraft like this one from Harrowbeer and nearby R.A.F. Roborough. Note that this aircraft is in it's original role as a torpedo carrying dive bomber. 691's aircraft were flown in the Army Co-operation Service.

The Squadron's Mascot?

This Spitfire, Vb, of No. 302 Polish Squadron may be ready for the next sortie, the pilot holding a small dog mascot to give him good luck and assurance on a hazardous flight over the English Channel or over enemy occupied Europe.

This informal photograph recalls an everyday scene at Harrowbeer when crews were on a 15 minute readiness position. Most of the nine personnel are wearing Mae West jackets relaxing and playing cards yet ready to go into action at a momemt's notice. Both photographs on this page show members of No. 193 Squadron. The four crew members below are also wearing life jackets seen here sometime in 1943. The stress and unexpectancy of undertaking flying missions must have weighed heavily on them in these brief moments of relaxation close to their living quarters.

A Spitfire, H.F. XII, of No. 131 Squadron, stands at Harrowbeer sometime between March and May, 1944. It was piloted by E. King.

The Hawker Typhoon 1b of No. 183 Squadron did service at this station from June to August, 1944. It had four cannons of 20mm and was powered by a Napier Sabre engine of 2,200 hp.

This Spitfire IXc of No. 126 Squadron, Mk126, 5 J-G, is equipped with a long range fuel tank as seen between the wheels. It had two 20mm cannons and four .303 machine guns.

Support for the Allied cause during the war came from many countries throughout the world. Here can be seen the Brazilian ambassador inspecting personnel at Harrowbeer, his country having paid for one of the Typhoon lined up for inspection. This took place on 21st September, 1943.

Harrowbeer often had many unusual visitors from other stations in the U.K. This Sea Otter, an amphibious biplane, flew into Harrowbeer and out the same day and was named *Michael* after the son of the pilot, R. Holman.

Senior Officers at R.A.F. Harrowbeer

Wing Commander J. Butterworth, C.O. of the station, is in the above photograph. He was in charge during 1943 and 1944. With him in the August, 1944, group are Sqn. Ldr. MacKenzie, C.O., No. 64 Squadron, and Sqn. Ldr. Plazis D.F.C., C.O. of No. 126 Sqn. The last two officers also stand in the lower group this time with Wing Commander H. Bird-Wilson.

The Duke of Kent is seen here with Czech pilots of Nos. 212 and 213 Squadrons. Their names have been inked in and their skill, daring and courage is helping to bring the war to an end will be remembered by British personnel who served with them at Harrowbeer.

This Typhoon of No. 193 Squadron flew from Harrowbeer. The pilot, wearing a life jacket, is pictured with ground staff sometime in 1943. The photograph below shows two crew dressed in their immersion suits which probably show they are about to fly on a mission over the English Channel. The plane is a Swordfish with No. 838 Squadron, Fleet Air Arm, with J. Steward, E. Townsend and William Locke smiling for the photographer.

Membership Card

This is to Certify that

P.O. (A) W.J. Locke

has qualified as a member of the Goldfish Club by escaping death by the use of his Emergency Dinghy on

July 6th, 1945.*

Signed ....

CHARLES A. ROBERTSON

Hon. Secretary

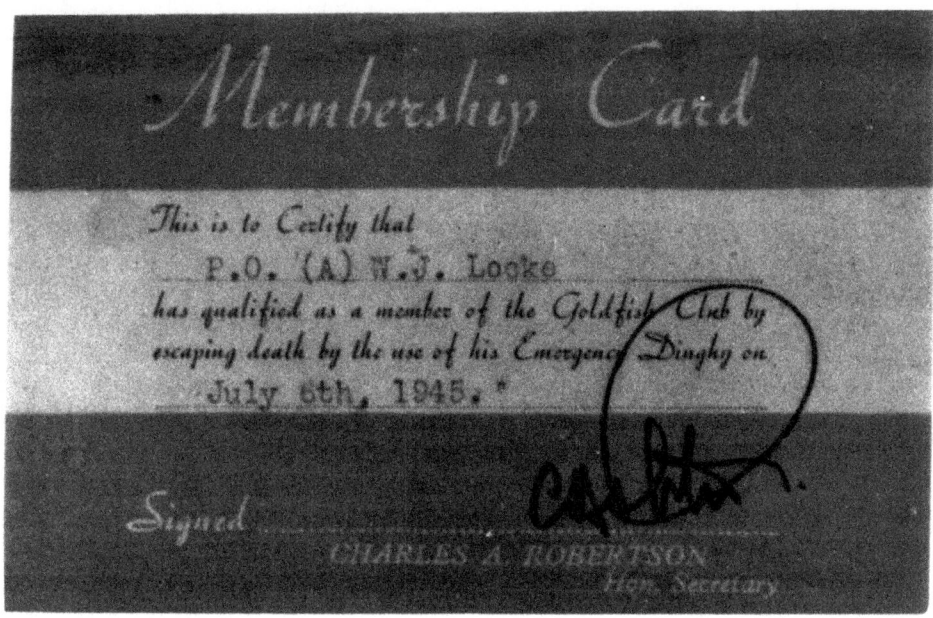

This membership of the *Goldfish Club* was awarded to personnel rescued from the sea after using an emergency dinghy. It is not known how many were rescued but a large part of the operations from the station was concerned with this work throughout most of the war.

A Rescue Celebration

Officers and other personnel of No. 276 Air Sea Rescue Squadron stand on the steps of *Ravenscroft*, the station's H.Q., in celebration of the 100th rescue of crew from the sea. This was a very important part of the role of the station.

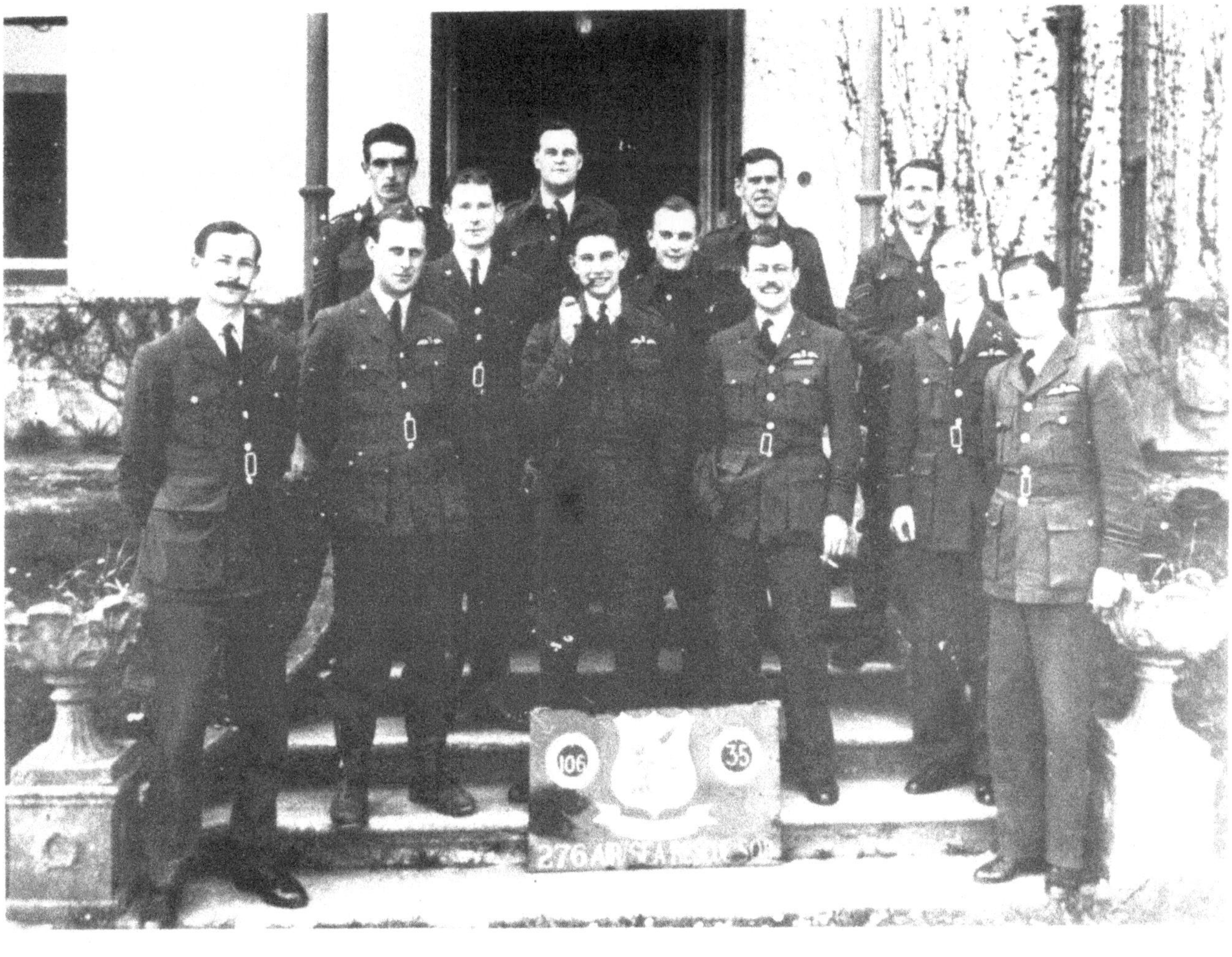

R.A.F. Harrowbeer, Yelverton, Devon.
1941 - 1949

R.A.F. Harrowbeer, Yelverton, Devon.
1941 - 1949

Supermarine Spitfire Mk Vb.
Nº 302 'Poznan' Squadron. R.A.F.
Free Polish Fighter Squadron.
Based at Harrowbeer, Devon.
November 1941 - May 1942.

Westland Lysander Mk III.
Nº 276 Squadron, Royal Air Force.
Air Sea Rescue Squadron.
Based at Harrowbeer, Devon.
October 1941 - May 1943.

R.A.F. Harrowbeer, Yelverton, Devon.
1941 - 1949

Supermarine Walrus Mk II.
Nº 276 Squadron, Royal Air Force.
Air Sea Rescue Squadron.
Formed at Harrowbeer, 21st October 1941,
and served there October 1941 - April 1944.

R.A.F. Harrowbeer, Yelverton, Devon.
1941 - 1949

Drawings by artist David Gibbings.

Hawker Typhoon Mk 1b
Nº 193 Squadron, Royal Air Force.
Formed at Harrowbeer December 1942.
The squadron operated from there
December 1942 - February 1944.

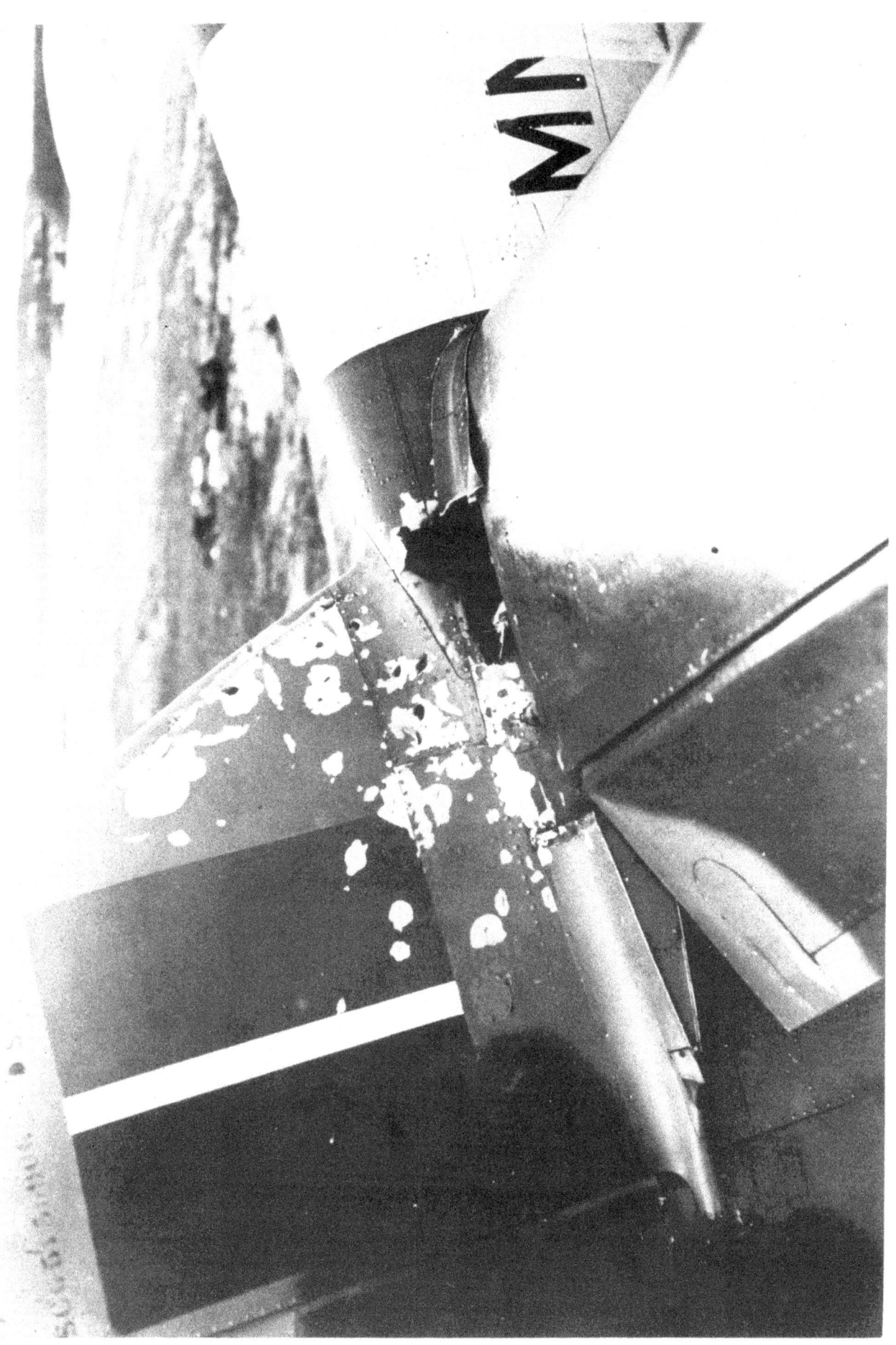

As was to be expected many of the Station's aircraft sustained varying degrees of damage while on sorties over France and the Channel Islands. Many were also lost with all crew killed or reported missing. This is the condition of the tail area of Wg. Cdr. Bird Wilson's Spitfire as a result of enemy fire over France.

D. C. Teague.

The above painting and lower photograph show two views of enemy shipping, the upper being a German "E" boat which was attacked in October, 1942, by Hurricane IIbs of No. 175 Squadron, in the English Channel. These fast speed boats could cause much havoc to naval movements. The photograph below was taken on board one of the German's convoys and clearly shows the very close formation these ships kept while steaming through the English Channel probably on route to or from their home port.

Arthur L. Clamp – the man behind the books

Arthur Leslie Clamp was a man of boundless energy with a passion for helping others, particularly through his love of history. A printer by trade, he started his career in a printing company before moving his family from Exeter to Plymouth to teach at the Plymouth College of Art and Design, where he eventually became the Head of the Printing Department.

A Devoted Family Man

Arthur with his five children.

Despite his love of teaching, Arthur prioritised his family, always making it home by 5:30pm for tea. He and his wife, Rosemary, raised five children: Susan, Angela, Elizabeth, David, and Steven. Arthur would often combine his love of family and history by taking his children on Sunday walks, encouraging them to appreciate historical monuments by taking photos or making crayon rubbings of gravestones for his books. The family home at 203 Elburton Road was a hub of activity, with a large garden, featuring a two-storey fort and a makeshift swimming pool.

A Lifelong Learner and Adventurer

Arthur's thirst for knowledge extended beyond history to a deep curiosity about the world. He was passionate about exploring different cultures, traditions, and cuisines, often taking advantage of his long summer holidays as a teacher to travel to places like India, Russia, South America, the middle east and the USA, sometimes bringing one of his children along. This adventurous spirit even influenced his home life, as seen by the short-lived family tradition of steam-cooking vegetables after a trip to Iceland.

History is a prominent feature of family days out

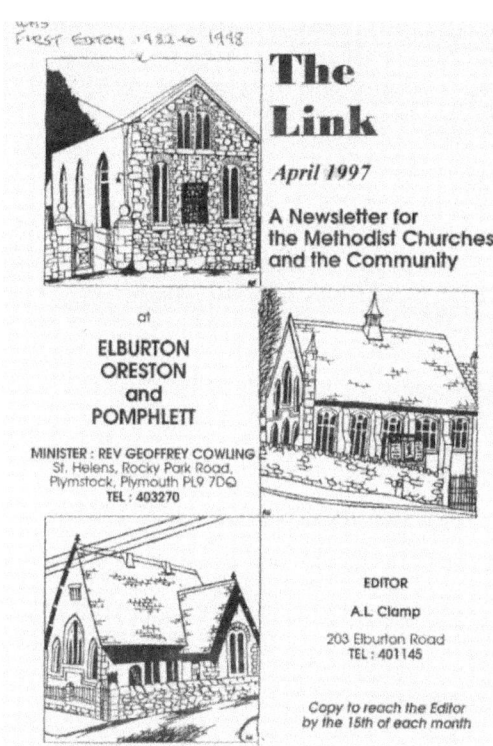

Community and Philanthropic Spirit

His commitment to serving others was evident in his long-standing involvement with the Elburton Methodist Church. He was the Sunday School Superintendent for over 15 years and served as the editor of the wider church's monthly newsletter, "The Link," for a similar duration. After Rosemary's very sad passing, Arthur later remarried and, following a chance encounter with a professor from India, established a connection with a missionary school in Chennai. Together with his new wife, Christine, he co-founded a "Sponsor a Child's Education" program that continues to this day.

Pictured left – The cover of 'The Link' complete with hand drawn sketches of each church by Angela
Below right – Arthur Clamp promoting his latest book
Below left – Arthur at home with his first wife, Rosemary
Below centre – Arthur on holiday with his second wife, Christine

A Legacy of Learning and Positivity

Arthur's greatest passion was history, which he brought to life through tireless research, documentation, and the many books he authored. He was driven by a need to "never be stuck in a rut," constantly seeking new experiences, meeting new people, and expanding his knowledge. With a positive attitude and a great sense of humour, he was always ready to help others, leaving a lasting impact on his family and community. His children, Susan, Angela, Elizabeth, David, and Steven, remember him with love and gratitude.

David Clamp, 2025

A Legacy of Local History

Below is the story of how Arthur L Clamp began writing books, in his own words, drafted shortly before he passed away in 2001. I have only made minor alterations to this text, correcting grammatical errors that he did not survive to correct himself. When I first discovered this text, I was shocked to see my name mentioned. It seems that, unbeknownst to me, I shared my first PC with him. I suspect he used it during the day when I was at school, although I do have one memory of sitting with him and showing him how it worked. It has been a pleasure to pick up where he left off and see his books republished and redistributed, and to know that I was part of the story, even back then. It was also fascinating to discover that his pricing structure matches the way I have tried to price the books, with a third going to local sellers and the rest covering printing costs with a little left over for my expenses.

I am his eldest grandson, and it is a privilege to curate his legacy, which we are calling 'The Clamp Collection'. The very last line of the text originally reads "The following pages list all the titles." Sadly, that page is missing and we have no record of all the books he published and knowing that some of those were researched by other authors makes the process of finding them even harder. I look forward to one day completing the collection and seeing them all available again. And maybe, one day, I'll even start writing my own to add to the series. For now, here is his story in his own words.

Steven Gibson, 2025

Writing and Publishing Booklets on Local Topics and Areas

I started this interest in either 1968 or 1969 when living in Woodford. I had by these dates established the Department of Printing and I think I must have been looking for something different to do. The first titles were of A5 size proofed from type set at Clarke, Doble and Brendon, Ltd., Plymouth printers, and then made up into pages and printed at Sawtell and Neilson, Ltd., Totnes.

Then began a slow process of getting them out to shops, etc. which proved to be more time consuming and difficult than actually researching, writing and getting the books into print. However, I persisted and opened a business account with Barclays Bank on the Broadway. I was advised to give it a title so I called it "Westway Publications". There came along another problem, one of storage of paper and finished books which was solved when the family moved to Elburton in 1970.

I changed the printer to Penwell, Ltd., Callington, Cornwall, as he was then just setting up himself and his prices seemed very reasonable. I did not get any of the printers to make up the complete books. I hand folded the flat printed sheets, stitched the books on a small manual table stitcher and trimmed them in a small hand turned guillotine which I bought from someone in Penzance for £40. It was brought up in a van.

The trouble and time going to and fro to Callington was too much so I transferred the printing to PDS Printers, Prince Rock, Plymouth, and I have been with them ever since. Now they are at Plympton which is easy to reach and they fold the flat sheets which was turning out to be a long chore which only saved a small part of the printing costs.

All my first titles were written by myself. I took the photographs and developed them in the loft of the house, the type was set by now on a computer situated in the house at Elburton from which I had collected photographic lengths of text to cut up and law down as pages.

At some point I decided that I would do my own film processing of lith film so I bought a large second hand process camera from Kingsbridge and learnt through trial and error to make line negatives of the text and halftone negatives of the illustrations which proved more difficult than I anticipated. The main problem was trying to keep the developer in the large dish at the correct temperature as any change would affect the developing time. I replaced this old camera with a brand new one bought from Croydon, Surrey, costing £900. This has turned out to be a great asset cutting out an expensive part of the printer's costs and one crucial aspect of the work which I could control.

By the middle 1970s there were many outlets I had contacted in Plymouth, up to Dartmoor, Exeter, around to Torbay, Totnes, Dartmouth and the South Hams. The market for local books was much greater than I had first thought and through getting to know many local people undertaking research themselves had the chance to help and make up books for other people who had in most instances, got together a collection of photographs with some text in a rather muddled way. Through my experience in print I was able to shape up their work and get it into print and in every case I had to pay the printer and let the person have the royalties. In the majority of titles produced in this manner this was another way of producing titles and it did give some profit to my work. However, I must say that in a few cases I lost out by either the other person getting the numbers wrong, not returning any monies from stock I delivered or they thought that more of their books should have been sold.

The print run was usually 1,000 copies and from time to time I have had reprints of 250 copies. It took about ten years to clear the first print run so I always had large stocks in the garage, workshop, etc. The numbers sold during the early years was about 7,000 copies a year increasing to around 9,000 copies and for the whole of the enterprise about 500,000 have been sold. The booklets have become part of the local scene and many people collect them, shops regularly order copies and I go around certain areas month by month restocking or replacing titles as necessary.

During the past year or so I have started setting the text on a Packard Bell PC, something which I should have done some years back. I share it with Steven Gibson, my grandson. There appears to be no end to the market for local books, but I could not earn a regular income because of the long time it takes to sell stock.

However, now exceeding 100 titles made up mainly of A4 twenty-four page booklets, some folded guides, with selling prices set with a third going to the shop which is the trade custom, the original idea has been quite successful and could go on for ever.

Apart from monetary benefits, however spasmodically these might be, I have learnt a lot myself, met many interesting people and have become part of the local scene with requests to give talks and to advise people about getting into print.

Arthur L Clamp, 2001

This newspaper article, published by the Evening Herald on 17th August 2001, forms a good record of his life. Just as he encourages us to learn more about local history, we encourage you to learn a little about him. For that reason, we have included these pages at the back of all the most recently republished books, in honour of his memory and recognition of his contribution to the community.

www.ingramcontent.com/pod-product-compliance
Lightning Source LLC
Chambersburg PA
CBHW061406070526
44584CB00031B/4171